Earthly Career & Heavenly Calling

PHILOMENA IKONAGBON

Syncterface Media
London
www.syncterfacemedia.com

Unless otherwise indicated, all Scripture quotations in this book are taken from the New King James Version of the Holy Bible, Copyright 1982 by Thomas Nelson, Inc. Quotations marked NIV are from the New International Version®, NIV® Copyright © 1973, 1978, 1984, 2011 by Biblica, Inc.
Quotations marked NLT are from the New Living Translation copyright© 1996, 2004, 2007 by Tyndale House Foundation.
Quotations marked NASB are from the New American Standard Bible Copyright © 1960, 1962, 1963, 1968, 1971, 1972, 1973, 1975, 1977, 1995 by The Lockman Foundation.
Quotations marked AMP are taken from the Amplified Bible, ©1954, 1958, 1962,1964, 1965, 1987 by The Lockman Foundation.

(Capitalised text and italics may be used for emphasis)
Used by permission.

No part of this book may be reproduced or transmitted in any form or by any means, graphic, electronic, or mechanical, including photocopying, recording, taping or by any information storage or retrieval system, without the permission of the author.

EARTHLY CAREER AND HEAVENLY CALLING
ISBN: 978-0-9569741-6-7
Copyright © April 2014
Philomena Ikonagbon
All Rights Reserved

Published in the United Kingdom by

Syncterface Media
London
www.syncterfacemedia.com
info@syncterfacemedia.com

Cover Design: Syncterface Media, London

This book is printed on acid-free paper

Contents

Acknowledgements v
Dedication vii
Preface ix
Foreword xi
Lay Up Treasures in Heaven 1
The Journey from the Beginning 5
Familiarity Breeds Contempt 11
Why did I listen? I should have stayed back 17
He is God and He does not change 21
Holy Spirit The Greatest Teacher 31
God's Will on Earth as it is in Heaven 37
The Reward 43
How Much Time do You Think You Have Left? 55
Be Rich Towards God, There Lies Your Guarantee 65
The Balancing Act 73

ACKNOWLEDGEMENTS

I am indebted to all the members of **Women of Faith Ministry**. You all have been so amazing. To Elo Anaro-Wood, you are a friend and a sister indeed. You have been an emblem of commitment and consistency.

My appreciation to all the members of **Faith Family Network** especially Mr & Mrs Boodram, Mr & Mrs Adelusi, Mr & Mrs Anaro-Wood, Adekemi Cassidy and Mrs Koleoso. I could not have run these ministries without your immense support. The joy of it all is that we have all grown to become one big family.

To Pastor & Mrs Kunle Raji, Pastor & Mrs Philip Membu and Evangelist Susan Noreen, your support in the ministry is highly appreciated. May the Lord continue to reward you.

To Pastor and Mrs Tony Okonmah, thank you so much for that initial proof reading of this book. May God richly bless you.

To all who have encouraged me over the years and supported me in this journey of life and ministry, I am indeed grateful.

Dedication

To the Almighty God, the Alpha and Omega.

To my wonderful husband, Courage Osaretin, who allowed me to serve God freely without restrictions, I love you.

To my children, Raphael and Valerie, you are a heritage from the Lord and the best gifts ever.

To my brothers and sisters including all my families far and wide, I could not have chosen differently.

To all my in-laws, you are the best.

To my precious mum, you will always remain forever in my heart.

PREFACE

As you read this book, may it enlighten you and transform your thinking on the subject of how our lives on earth can determine what our rewards would be in heaven.

My prayer is that, as you set your mind on things above and not on things on the earth (Colossians 3:2), may your work not be in vain and when you get to heaven, may you hear, 'well done thou good and faithful servant' in Jesus Christ Name, Amen.

Philomena Ikonagbon

Foreword

This book is a true reflective story of divine appointment with destiny (for those who believe in destiny) as narrated by the author which can benefit everyone irrespective of faith obligations. The simplicity of narration, flare of transparent unadulterated incidents and accounts told with captivating honesty, makes "Earthly Career and Heavenly Calling" a highly recommended read for Christians who requires God's direction in the affairs of their lives.

It is a great book for Christian evangelism. A highly recommended sermon book for preachers and ministers. Above all, it is a wakeup call for every Christian who desires to make heaven. I found chapter 6 the most compelling read. The analysis of the health insurance and pension contribution mechanisms and the correlation with the expectations of our assignments on earth is mind blowing.

This book is a work of love.

Pastor Tony Okonmah
Author, The Lies of Honest Men

1
LAY UP TREASURES IN HEAVEN

[19] "Do not lay up for yourselves treasures on earth, where moth and rust destroy and where thieves break in and steal; [20] but lay up for yourselves treasures in heaven, where neither moth nor rust destroys and where thieves do not break in and steal.
[21] For where your treasure is, there your heart will be also.
[22] "The lamp of the body is the eye. If therefore your eye is good, your whole body will be full of light.
[23] But if your eye is bad, your whole body will be full of darkness. If therefore the light that is in you is darkness, how great is that darkness!
[24] "No one can serve two masters; for either he will hate the one and love the other, or else he will be loyal to the one and despise the other. You cannot serve God and mammon.

Matthew 6:19-24

I laid on my bed one Saturday morning reminiscing on my life and some setbacks I had experienced. One thought that was most pressing on my mind was whether I had made the right choice in the career I had chosen. Even though I was already past my youth, I began to analyse the various options available to me and I toyed with the idea of changing my career to a much more 'seemingly' lucrative one. As far as

I was concerned, all that actually mattered was the remuneration. I thought to myself, 'if I could just change my career and earn a 'fat' salary, meeting my basic needs, which was increasingly becoming a challenge, would not be a concern. If nothing else, that would leave me with fewer issues to worry about. However, I must say that, even in all of my thoughts, I could sense the voice of the Holy Spirit ministering words of comfort to my spirit.

The Lord knows it all

> [1] *You have searched me, Lord, and you know me.*
> [2] *You know when I sit and when I rise; you perceive my thoughts from afar.*
> [3] *You discern my going out and my lying down; you are familiar with all my ways.*
> [4] *Before a word is on my tongue you, Lord, know it completely.*
> [5] *You hem me in behind and before, and you lay your hand upon me.*
> [6] *Such knowledge is too wonderful for me, too lofty for me to attain*
>
> Psalms 139:1-6 (NIV)

Still on my bed and not knowing which way to turn, I started to have a deeper sense, in my heart, of the whispers of the Holy Spirit in a way no human would ever have done. He began to teach me the basic principles of life as it relates to my career and the calling God has placed over my life while here on earth.

What I am about to share with you in this book are the teachings of the Holy Spirit to me as He ministered to my heart on that fateful morning. I believe it will bless you because it has, indeed, changed my perception about life and helped me create a balance between an earthly career and a heavenly calling. I am confident these principles will change your world and revolutionise your thinking too.

So, sit back, relax and let me take you on the journey that resulted in the birth of this book. As you read, may the Holy Spirit, who is the greatest teacher of all times, minister to your spirit, soul and body and may He unravel the mind of God to you on the issue of your earthly career and heavenly calling.

2
THE JOURNEY FROM THE BEGINNING

[21] *There are many plans in a man's heart, Nevertheless the Lord's counsel—that will stand.*

Proverbs 19:21

Growing up in Africa, I had developed a passion for journalism and law. My intention was to study one of these courses. However, as fate would have it, due to lack of funds, my dreams did not materialise as I had hoped. Having lost my dad at a very tender age, my siblings and I were raised singlehandedly by our mum. As a result, I had no hope of actualising my dream and thought my passion and dream had gone down the drain. But most true is the scriptures in the book of Proverbs that says that, *"a man's heart plans his way, But the LORD directs his steps"* (Proverbs 16:9). This verse described, accurately, the case in my life.

You might call it fate, chance or destiny; Eventually, I ended up becoming a Secretary. Although it was way out of what I wanted to become in life, the only real option that presented itself to me was that of being a secretary. Little did I know that becoming a secretary was a blessing in disguise. You may be wondering why I felt this way. Well, I will tell you. When I got married and joined my husband in Vienna, the only job I would consider decent that was available to me was a secretarial role. Having gotten the job, I was now tagged as 'one of the luckiest persons' among my peers because I had this so called 'decent job.' The norm was to take on meagre jobs just to get-by because the so called 'decent jobs' were not readily available for migrants particularly those classed as ethnic minorities.

Others may call it luck but I choose to call it divine destiny. Unknown to me, the Most High, being an awesome God, the One who knows the beginning from the end, had prepared me well in advance for where I was going long before I knew it. God's promises concerning me became evident in one of my favourite passages of the bible in Jeremiah 29:11 that says, '**For I know the plans I have for you," declares the Lord, "plans to prosper you and not to harm you, plans to give you hope and a future.**' God knew that studying any other course would not have been useful at that initial stage of my life. I eventually worked as a secretary in Vienna for over eight years earning a reasonable salary before finally relocating to the United Kingdom.

Relocate! Do we really have to?

If you were in my shoes, living in a land where working as a secretary seems the best option available to you, I am sure you would understand my frustrations when my husband decided all of a sudden that it was time for us to relocate to the United Kingdom. Our relocation plan did not make sense at the time to anyone because no one in their right senses would dream of leaving certainty for uncertainty. The truth of the matter was, to a great extent, we were comfortable and there was really no need to relocate to anywhere. The second amazing thing about our relocation frenzy was the fact that my job had an associated incentive which included a significant lump sum payment if you resigned after more than ten years service, which, at this point, I had not attained. So it didn't really make sense that I was about to give up all of these just to relocate. In the human way of reasoning, the best approach would have been to work and accumulate the minimum ten year requirement period and if for any reason we were still adamant on relocating, then I will not lose out on the incentive package. But, here was I, being commanded by the love of my life (my husband) to leave everything I held dearly and relocate with the whole family to the United Kingdom.

At this point of my life, I was now dithering between staying behind to complete the ten year requirement for the incentive package or take the risk by resigning and lose out on everything just to obey my husband's command. This whole process of deciding whether to stay or go made me remember the account of Abraham – our Father - in Genesis 12:1-3 when God told him to leave everything he was familiar with and go to an unfamiliar ground. I then thought to myself, really and truly, it must have been a very difficult decision for Abraham to make. The bible records that Abraham obeyed God. At that point in time, I didn't have the kind of faith Abraham must have had. No wonder Abraham was being referred to in the bible as the 'Father of Faith.' I tried to comprehend my inability to make an apt decision and sometimes wondered and even questioned whether it was lack of faith on my part or simply fear of the unknown then I remembered this passage in the

Bible in Genesis 15:6 that says, '**And Abram believed the Lord, and the Lord counted him as righteous because of his faith**'. In my case, I began to contemplate whether this was God.

Obedience! When it is not even convenient

> *¹ The Lord had said to Abram, "Go from your country, your people and your father's household to the land I will show you.*
> *² "I will make you into a great nation, and I will bless you; I will make your name great, and you will be a blessing.*
> *³ I will bless those who bless you, and whoever curses you I will curse; and all peoples on earth will be blessed through you."*
>
> Genesis 12:1-3 (NIV)

Prior to this time, even though my husband did not visit often, I had always visited the United Kingdom at every opportunity. You can now understand why I was in a state of shock when he decided all of a sudden to go for further studies in the United Kingdom. Whilst I was amenable to this, a complete relocation with the entire family was something I did not bargain for at the time. To me, as long as he was not expecting me to leave my job and go with him, I was comfortable because he could simply leave us behind, go for his studies, complete his course and return. However, being a conventional family man that he is, my husband had a different view. He didn't think it was a wise idea to relocate alone to the United Kingdom while we stayed behind. His model idea of family is staying together at all times through thick or thin but the whole idea of relocating gave me sleepless nights.

Having overcome the initial resentment, I had come to love Vienna and made good friends both in Church and at work and did not find any justification for relocating. As the saying often goes, "if it isn't broken, don't fix it". During the whole process, I felt like I was being uprooted like a tree and was deeply concerned for the future.

3
FAMILIARITY BREEDS CONTEMPT

> [4] *When He had stopped speaking, He said to Simon, "Launch out into the deep and let down your nets for a catch."*
> [5] *But Simon answered and said to Him, "Master, we have toiled all night and caught nothing; nevertheless at Your word I will let down the net."*
> [6] *And when they had done this, they caught a great number of fish, and their net was breaking.*
>
> Luke 5:4-6

In most cases, our familiarity with places or things can impact us positively or negatively. We usually form our opinions long before we truly have personal experiences of them. The result is always that we resent or take things for granted even before we have the full information or knowledge. We could become so stereotypical to the extent that we refuse to budge when new ideas or opportunities are being presented to us through the help of the Holy Spirit.

This reminds me of the story of Simon Peter, one of the disciples of Jesus Christ narrated in Luke 5:1-11. Simon being an experienced fisherman, along with some other men, had toiled all night fishing but they caught nothing. I couldn't imagine how they felt when Jesus came and told them, "**Launch out into the deep and let down your nets for a catch**" (Luke 5:4-5). It is no surprise therefore that Simon responded in such manner in verse 5 when he said, "**Master, we have toiled all night and caught nothing; nevertheless at Your word I will let down the net.**" He was confident he was an experienced fisherman who knew when, where and how to throw the net when fishing. To him, this was his profession and very familiar ground and needed no lessons on the subject of fishing, especially not from someone who was a carpenter.

The amazing thing about this story is that despite his opinion on the matter, through the wisdom of the Holy Spirit, he went ahead and launched out into the deep at the Lord's command. The result of this obedience was that Peter caught so much fish that his net was breaking and he had to call on his partners for help in taking in the catch. His previous experience almost robbed him of a great catch. Have you had any previous bitter experience that is hindering you from taking another bold step forward? My prayer for you is that, despite your previous experiences, you would learn to trust God again from today onwards, in Jesus Name. Amen.

Get rid of that negative mindset – Trust Him

> [1] *"Thus says the Lord to His anointed, To Cyrus, whose right hand I have held— To subdue nations before him*
> *And loose the armor of kings, To open before him the double doors, So that the gates will not be shut:*
> [2] *'I will go before you And make the crooked places[a] straight; I will break in pieces the gates of bronze And cut the bars of iron.*
> [3] *I will give you the treasures of darkness And hidden riches of secret places, That you may know that I, the Lord,*

Who call you by your name, Am the God of Israel.

Isaiah 45:1-3

As stated earlier, previous visits to the United Kingdom gave me the opportunity to acquaint myself with the general lifestyle of the people and places I visited. In my opinion, I concluded that it was okay for me to visit but certainly not a place I would wish to live. I felt it was a fast-paced country and indeed too fast for my liking. A glimpse at people's daily busy schedule scared me out of my wits. I thought it was the norm for everyone to take on more than one job or put in extra hours of work in order to survive. On the contrary, Vienna was a very relaxed city despite other challenges.

It is okay to seek wise counsel

¹⁴ Where there is no counsel, the people fall;
But in the multitude of counselors there is safety.

Proverbs 11:14

I discussed the relocation process with my Pastor at the time, who, after listening to my concerns, advised me to take it to God in prayer because, if indeed it was His will, He could make smooth the pathway. He continued by saying, 'the idea will fizzle out and your husband will simply have a change of heart if God is not involved'. As I listened to his advice, I couldn't really help but hope and wish that the whole process would just go away.

In truth, throughout the discussion process, it dawned on me that I had never actually thought of praying about it or asking God for direction and instead I had just constantly complained about the situation. The fact that I did not wish to relocate gave me a reason not to pray. In my opinion, you only pray about what you want not what you don't want or wish.

Isn't that what we often do, complaining and moaning about anything and everything. How this or that is not working to anyone who cares to listen. It is only when all else fails that we remember to turn to God for help. We tend to make the first last and the last first when in reality it should be the other way round. Our God alone has the answer to any question we have or will ever have and He is always willing to show us the way out of any situation. I love the scriptures in Jeremiah 33:3 which says, **'Call to Me and I will answer you, and I will tell you great and mighty things, which you do not know'.** God is our ever available friend who is always ready and willing to help us in times of need if only we will learn to run to Him in any given situation. He is willing and able to make all the crooked places straight for us before we even arrive there.

If God said it and you believe it then...

> *[13] Now all Judah, with their little ones, their wives, and their children, stood before the Lord.*
>
> *[14] Then the Spirit of the Lord came upon Jahaziel the son of Zechariah, the son of Benaiah, the son of Jeiel, the son of Mattaniah, a Levite of the sons of Asaph, in the midst of the assembly.*
>
> *[15] And he said, "Listen, all you of Judah and you inhabitants of Jerusalem, and you, King Jehoshaphat! Thus says the Lord to you: 'Do not be afraid nor dismayed because of this great multitude, for the battle is not yours, but God's.*
>
> *2 Chronicles 20:13-15*

When I realised that my husband was adamant about relocating to the United Kingdom, I reluctantly decided to pray a lackadaisical prayer asking God for His will for us and the relocation plan. Amazingly, the merciful God did not consider my unbelief. He went ahead of us to execute His divine plan and did what He alone could do by creating a pathway for us. Ultimately, the aspiration to be an obedient wife despite all odds took the better of me.

One thing we must be clear about is this, the fact that we heard God and obeyed His instruction on any particular issue does not automatically remove all obstacles on the way. The good news is, because we know we heard God and we are following His instructions in obedience, it gives us the confidence and peace of mind we need for the entire journey ahead of us. When we believe and trust God, we are guaranteed victory in whatever battle we may face. We only need to keep standing while the Lord is fighting our battle. The only assignment for us is to believe in the Almighty God and trust Him all the way.

I love this passage in the bible in the book of Psalms 46:10, it says **"Be still and know that I am God..."** It means I don't have to fret about anything; all I need to do is remember He is God. This was the reason why when the people of Moab, Ammon and the rest invaded Judah in the book of 2 Chronicles 20, Jehoshaphat simply cried out to the Lord and the Lord, through His prophet Jahaziel, reminded the people that they need not be afraid for the battle is not theirs but God's.

So all we need to be aware of as children of God is that the battles we face on earth are not ours but God's. We only need to obey His commandments, stand still and remember He is the Almighty God. This does not mean we will never doubt at some point. Certainly not, but how do we handle our doubts? Do we simply sit back and allow doubts to take over our lives or do we run to God for grace and strength to stand in faith? These are choices you and I would have to make on a daily basis in every challenging situation we face. Whatever the case may be, I can guarantee you that if you hand anything over to God without doubting His abilities, He will surely take care of it.

4
WHY DID I LISTEN? I SHOULD HAVE STAYED BACK

> [11] They said to Moses, "Was it because there were no graves in Egypt that you brought us to the desert to die? What have you done to us by bringing us out of Egypt?
> [12] Didn't we say to you in Egypt, 'Leave us alone; let us serve the Egyptians'? It would have been better for us to serve the Egyptians than to die in the desert!"
>
> Exodus 14:11-12 (NIV)

The first few months after relocation were problematic. I had difficulties adjusting to the system; weather, irregular train times, not to mention the configuration of the rooms which were very small in sizes when compared to the bigger accommodations in Vienna. I felt squeezed on every side and I could not stop reminiscing on how good it was back in Vienna to the extent that I felt like returning.

In retrospect, my situation could be likened to what happened after God delivered the Israelites from bondage in Egypt as they were being led by Moses. The bible recalls in Exodus 14 that after God had delivered them from their task master, they complained against Moses about almost everything and anything and despite God's miraculous deeds; parting the red sea for their safe passage, feeding them with manna from Heaven, providing water from the rock, delivering them from the serpents and many more, they wished they had been left to die in Egypt and were ungrateful. The truth of the matter was, the children of Israel shifted their focus from God to material needs. As long as we focus on our circumstances and situation, we will remain frustrated but the moment we shift our focus to God, things will definitely change for the better.

Where was my focus?, On the problem or on God?

> [1] *Therefore we also, since we are surrounded by so great a cloud of witnesses, let us lay aside every weight, and the sin which so easily ensnares us, and let us run with endurance the race that is set before us,*
> [2] *looking unto Jesus, the author and finisher of our faith, who for the joy that was set before Him endured the cross, despising the shame, and has sat down at the right hand of the throne of God.*
> [3] *For consider Him who endured such hostility from sinners against Himself, lest you become weary and discouraged in your souls.*
>
> *Hebrews 12:1-3*

In spite of my faithlessness, God remained faithful. To enable you understand the Mercy of God upon our lives and how God truly went ahead to prepare the way for us, the Almighty God created an opportunity by providing me a job in an unusual way. Having shared my relocation dilemma with a sister-in-law living in the United Kingdom, I was advised to apply for an opening that was advertised. I obliged and was eventually offered the position. To further buttress the goodness of God, the resumption date was left open for me to decide when suitable. His mercy did not end at this. By divine connection, we got accommodation for a considerable number of months without any rent payment. After these miraculous provisions, I did not need any convincing that indeed, God had been involved all along. Despite this, there were still challenges, trials and hurdles settling in. Occasionally, the idea of returning would come to mind.

Mood swings!

> *⁵ "If you have raced with men on foot and they have worn you out, how can you compete with horses?*
> *If you stumble in safe country, how will you manage in the thickets by the Jordan?*
>
> *Jeremiah 12:5 (NIV)*

Eventually, we had to leave the accommodation for an uncomfortable temporary place, waiting to be re-housed. As the waiting period became protracted, the thought of returning to Vienna would sometimes creep in again. But God in His infinite wisdom would give me a Word from the scriptures. On one of those occasions, He directed me to the book of Jeremiah 12:5 that says, **"If you have raced with men on foot and they have worn you out, how can you compete with horses? If you stumble in safe country, how will you manage in the thickets by the Jordan?"** God in His unfailing mercy comforted me daily through His Word and made me understand that giving up on minor issues such as a place to live in, means confronting bigger matters when they do come in the future will be more challenging. My advice is to always find the right scripture for your situation and hold on to it.

Whilst our challenges are sometimes considered by others as small, to us they usually seem enormous. As we walk with God, we will gradually come to the realisation that it is never a problem for God to take care of our challenges. The truth is, God allows every issue or challenge we face to become a foundation and a building block for where He is taking us. It is so interesting because God may not show us the bigger picture or the end result of our assignment, but He may sometimes show us a glimpse. However, if we walk in faith and obey His commandments, He promised to take us step by step until we arrive at the final destination of our purpose. Trusting God is a key part of walking with God.

5
HE IS GOD AND HE DOES NOT CHANGE

⁶ *"For I am the Lord, I do not change; Therefore you are not consumed, O sons of Jacob.*

Malachi 3:6

God meets us wherever we are at. He is God and therefore patient and kind. He wants us to be happy. He wants the best for us and will never leave us in the dark. His thoughts towards us are thoughts of good and not of evil. The scriptures in Jeremiah 29:11 sums it all, **'For I know the thoughts that I think toward you, says the Lord, thoughts of peace and not of evil, to give you a future and a hope'**. God's desire is to bring us to that original place where He has always wanted us to be. This is what He makes us to understand in Deuteronomy 31:8 where He reminds us that He is the One who goes before us. He promised to be with us, never to leave nor forsake us. What an awesome promise! All we need do is, stop that fear before it stops us and put an end to that discouragement because He who promised is faithful. No matter how insignificant our questions or needs may appear to others, God will not trivialise them. If only we can trust Him enough to believe He hears and responds to our calls. He is the same God that said in His Word *'Call upon me in the day of trouble; I will deliver you and you shall glorify Me. '*(Psalms 50:15). Why not try and call on Him now for any challenge you might be facing today. He is no respecter of persons. He will always answer all who call upon His Name. He is well able to do all He has promised.

To enable me to see and understand clearly what His love means, the Holy Spirit painted for me a scenario of a child playing with a toy. If for any reason the toy gets broken, lost or stolen, the child would weep profusely until his parents are prepared to listen. Meanwhile, an adult may wonder why the child is weeping over a mere toy or ask, 'what is important in a toy?' To an adult, it is only a toy but to the child, it is the most precious and priceless possession. Usually, all it takes to pacify the child is a simple promise from the parents to repair or replace the toy, giving the child something to hold on to and hope for.

We are just like this little child in the eyes of God. Assuming this earthly parent can be trusted to fulfil their promise then the child has nothing to worry about. If the parents of this child who are human could be trusted, we ought to have more confidence in God. This is why Jesus Christ said in Matthew 7:11 and Luke 11:13 that *'if you then being evil, know how to give good gifts to your children, how much more will your heavenly Father give the Holy Spirit to those who ask Him'* The interesting thing is our heavenly Father cannot even be compared with our earthly parents when it comes to promises and the ability to fulfil them.

The Bible in Psalms 138 verse 2b makes us understand

that God honours His word more than His Name and 2 Corinthians 1:20 reminds us that all the promises of God in Christ are yea – meaning shall all be certainly fulfilled – and amen meaning true, faithful and certain – to the glory of God through us. How do you take God's word? Do you trust Him enough to believe His promises?

Sometimes our earthly parents, despite their love for us, do make promises that due to unforeseen circumstances, are not able to keep them. In Isaiah 49:16 the bible says, **"Can a mother forget the baby at her breast and have no compassion on the child she has borne? Though she may forget, I will not forget you!"** Our heavenly Father has given us that assurance that even though it is possible for our earthly parents to forget us, He will not forget us. Since it is impossible for God to lie in His word and promises (through Jesus Christ), this then makes our assurance of the fulfilment of His promises doubly sure (Hebrews 6:18). God is the same yesterday, today and forever. He does not change. His promises are sure.

Likewise, our heavenly Father wants us to have this type of hope without any iota of doubt just like the child I described. God will always give us a word concerning our circumstances if we ask Him and that word becomes the anchor of our hope throughout our trying period. Even though our expectations have not yet manifested, we just need to hold on - by faith - to what God has promised in His word. This was exactly what Apostle Paul talked about when he wrote in one of his epistles to the Romans saying '**....hope that is seen is not hope; for why does one still hope for what he sees? But if we hope for what we do not see, we eagerly wait for it with perseverance**' (Romans 8:24-25).

See the bigger picture

> *⁸ It was by faith that Abraham obeyed when God called him to leave home and go to another land that God would give him as his inheritance. He went without knowing where he was going.*
> *⁹ And even when he reached the land God promised him, he lived there by faith—for he was like a foreigner, living in tents. And so did Isaac and Jacob, who inherited the same promise.*
> *¹⁰ Abraham was confidently looking forward to a city with eternal foundations, a city designed and built by God.*
>
> Hebrews 11:8-10 (NLT)

In the same vein, our faith is renewed when God gives us a Word for our situation. That word becomes the foundation and bedrock of our hope in Him. It becomes the anchor of our soul - Hebrews 6:19 - because we know and believe that God cannot lie (Hebrews 6:18). We can then hold on to that Word we have heard in the place of prayer and in His word until we arrive at the destination that has been preordained by God. We must understand that God had a divine plan for each and every one of us long before we were born. As we can see in Jeremiah 1:5, when God spoke to Jeremiah and said, **"Before I formed you in the womb I knew you, before you were born I set you apart; I appointed you as a prophet to the nations."** It is clear that we did not just come to this earth as happenstance. We all have a purpose and an assignment to fulfil. Everything we do or go through in life forms the building block that leads us to that final assignment or destination provided we diligently obey His voice.

So it was in the case of Abraham when God told him in Genesis 12:1-3 and Hebrews 11:8-10 to leave his country to an unknown land. Abraham, the father of faith obeyed God and it was through the eyes of faith he saw clearly the Promise Land. God did not call Abraham just for the sake of it. He called him because He had a plan and purpose for Abraham and his entire generation. We are part of this generation because we are Abraham's seed. Galatians 3:29 says, *'And if you are Christ's, then you are Abraham's seed, and heirs according to the promise'*. It is only through the eyes of faith we can foresee our Promise Land. Paul encouraged us in his letter to the Galatians when he said, *'Let us not become weary in doing good, for at the proper time we will reap a harvest if we do not give up '*(Galatians 6:9). My prayer for you is that you don't get to that point in your life where you give up, thinking God is never going to do what you are asking or seeking Him for. All I can say is, don't ever give up on God because He will never give up on you. If He made a promise to you, He will fulfil it no matter how long it takes.

It is very important for us to find His word concerning our situation and hold on to it because it is the key to our breakthrough. Nobody can find it for you. Not even pastors or prophets can find out God's will for you. The duty of pastors or prophets is to guide you to the word of God. Ultimately, the responsibility still lies with you to seek Him. You must seek God for yourself and find out what His purpose for your life is and after you have found it, you must hold on to that promise and *war* with it until it is fulfilled. Paul charged Timothy to wage the good warfare concerning the prophecies that were made before him (1 Timothy 1:18). It is not enough to discover your purpose, you must also be prepared to wage a good warfare and not rest until you see the manifestation. The amazing thing about a good warfare is that Jesus Christ has already won the battle and victory for us is sure. Our only responsibility is to stand strong in that battle ground until it is over. My life and that of my family have been a living example of God's faithfulness. It was only through faith and obedience we were able to overcome.

Faith and Obedience – The bridge to your Promise Land

> *[13] For when God made a promise to Abraham, because He could swear by no one greater, He swore by Himself,*
> *[14] saying, "Surely blessing I will bless you, and multiplying I will multiply you."*
> *[15] And so, after he had patiently endured, he obtained the promise.*
>
> Hebrews 6:13-15

Abraham was a man that truly obeyed God in every respect. Once God said it, Abraham without a doubt was willing and ready to obey. In like manner, God wants us to get to that point where we will trust Him totally with every issue of our lives.

To prove the certainty of God's Word, we were eventually settled into our own home. I successfully, even as a mature student, completed a law degree and gradually, things began to fall into place. Having read the scriptures and various accounts of men and women on their journey through life with God, it is clear that they all made a conscious decision to believe God's report rather than the prevailing circumstance. We must also make a decision on whose report we choose to believe, whether is the report of the circumstance presenting itself before us or the report of our Lord Jesus Christ which we can only see through 'the eyes of faith'. In my case, I had a choice; I could either focus on our situation and be discouraged or focus on God and be encouraged. I had to choose the latter even though it wasn't easy at first.

Similarly, in Numbers chapters 13 and 14 we are told in the scriptures that God told Moses to send men to go and spy out the land of Canaan, a land He was about to give to the children of Israel. Moses eventually sent out twelve spies and told them to see what the land was like, whether the people there were weak or strong, few or many, whether the land was good or bad and whether the land was rich or poor. The people actually went up and spied out the land. However, when they returned after forty days, even though they came back with the fruit of the land, ten of them said *"...we are not able to go up against the people, for they are stronger than we."* (Numbers 13:31). The spies further frightened the children of Israel by saying the people living in that land are giants and that they were like grasshoppers in their own eyes. The spies could only see the giants in the land because that was where their focus was – the obstacles. They failed to see the fruits of the land – God's promises and His blessings thereof. Amazingly, only Joshua and Caleb looked beyond the giants in the land. They were the only two who were confident enough to trust God and believe His word that, the same God who spoke to Moses and told him to send spies to the land is also able to give them the land. Joshua and Caleb through the eyes of faith said to the people *"...let us go up at once and take possession, for we are well able to overcome it"* (Numbers 13 vs 30).

There is nothing much we can do in the Kingdom of God without faith. Faith is the currency of the Kingdom of God and the bible makes this very clear in Hebrews 11:6 *"...And it is impossible to please God without faith. Anyone who wants to come to Him must believe that*

God exists and that He rewards those who sincerely seek Him". Do you trust God enough to believe His word and promises?

Isn't it true that as humans, we tend to focus more and complain about the negatives rather than drawing inspiration from the positives? The truth of the matter is, if we will concentrate on the positives, the negatives would eventually shrink. If we learn to recall the goodness of God in our lives and praise Him daily for those things we sometimes take for granted, then our 'giant' problems would disappear before we know it. In the end, we will be able to focus on what God would rather have us do on earth. Recognising the devices of the enemy and his agenda to shift our focus away from the original plans of God is important. Otherwise, we become entangled with earthly issues to the detriment of our God-given assignment.

Count your blessings daily

> *5 Why am I discouraged? Why is my heart so sad?*
> *I will put my hope in God!*
> *I will praise him again — my Savior and my God!*
>
> Psalms 43:5 (NLT)

I began to reflect on our journey and how God had brought us thus far and I could not help but count my blessings. How I miraculously got my first job before I even remembered to pray about it and a house before I asked Him for one. Not to mention His faithfulness throughout my time when studying for a law degree. My faith within me rose to another level and I began to listen to the voice of the Holy Spirit whispering to my innermost being, just the way He had done in the past. As the Holy Spirit took me through various thoughts and brought to my remembrance countless victories of the past, I began to reflect and focus more on what really matters most in life – the heavenly assignment.

The Holy Spirit spoke clearly to my heart that I do not need to worry or bother about changing my career. He reminded me that all I needed to do was get myself ready for the remaining exams because success was already mine. He reminded me that the most important things in life are not earthly careers but heavenly callings. He then began to teach me the difference between earthly careers and heavenly callings. It was only after this revelation that I found true joy in my situation.

6
HOLY SPIRIT
THE GREATEST TEACHER

[18] *"And you shall remember the Lord your God, for it is He who gives you power to get wealth, that He may establish His covenant which He swore to your fathers, as it is this day.*

Deuteronomy 8:18

Before I talk about earthly careers and heavenly callings, I would like to narrate an interesting experience I had with the Holy Spirit. After my degree, I went straight into law school. On one occasion, I sat for one of the exams which I thought, at the time, was the most difficult examination I had ever undertaken. Of course, it turned out to be so because I had already conceded to defeat through my thoughts and my words. Proverbs 18:21 says, *'Death and life are in the power of the tongue. And those who love it will eat its fruit'*. You can imagine how I felt when I realised I had failed, meaning I needed to prepare and retake this dreadful exam. To say I was very unhappy is an understatement and I was really scared of having to do this all over again. I questioned God on why I was not successful on first attempt despite my service and devotion to His cause. I felt like a failure. However The Holy Spirit made me understand, in clear terms, the heavenly definition of the word – success - and I will share it with you.

The Holy Spirit said to me, "Success is not about everything you decide to do. Success is about all that I have called you to do. It is about the Kingdom of God, His will and purpose being accomplished through you. He said, that is what I call SUCCESS." The Holy Spirit continued, 'Success is not finishing or passing an examination set by men but success is about accomplishing the assignment or examination given by God.' In clear terms, the Holy Spirit began to minister to my heart, reminding me that He is the Greatest Teacher and He decides whether a man has passed or failed in life. He is the one that marks the greatest examination or tests anybody has or will ever take on earth. He gives the scores and awards the marks. Also, He alone knows the pass mark for every man or woman on the face of the earth. The Holy Spirit continued by reminding me that no one else can mark or award me any certificate without His approval. He said that no one can award His own kind of certificates and rewards. He continued by reminding me that, His rewards for each one cannot be measured neither do we know how the marks are awarded. He said, "Believe Me, I am the Greatest Teacher"

This was really an eye opener for me. The Holy Spirit was simply teaching me that if passing an examination set by men was all I needed in life, He would have handed it to me on a platter but I needed more than that. From that point on, I realised that it was not just about my law exams, it was more of a training ground, a foundational lesson and a life changing experience God wanted me to understand and grasp. A lifelong lecture needed for my future and for where He was taking me. I realised that God wanted me to learn tenacity and patience. I needed the experience of being able to persevere and the faith to hold on to God's word no matter the circumstances. Tenacity and patience are not things you learn theoretically, you need the personal experiences to bring out these qualities.

Stand still, remember He is still God

> [31] *"Therefore do not worry, saying, 'What shall we eat?' or 'What shall we drink?' or 'What shall we wear?'*
> [32] *For after all these things the Gentiles seek. For your heavenly Father knows that you need all these things.*
> [33] *But seek first the kingdom of God and His righteousness, and all these things shall be added to you.*
>
> Matthew 6:31-33

It is natural for us to class people as being successful based on their material wealth and the possessions we see. However, God sees things differently. In Isaiah 55:8 God made it clear to us when He said, "**For my thoughts are not your thoughts, neither are your ways my ways, says the LORD**". While we tend to look at the outward appearance, God looks at the heart (1 Samuel 16:7). The state of our heart and our work towards our heavenly assignment is what matters to God.

After that beautiful lecture in the 'School of the Holy Spirit' on the meaning of success, I didn't need anyone to tell me or remind me not to worry any longer about my law school exams, I knew right there and then that everything about me, including my career aspirations, needed to be handed over to the Greatest Teacher who will mark and reward me at the end of everything here on earth.

Let me be honest, while I was in Law School, because of the intensity and volume of the workload, my focus shifted more towards my school work rather than the assignment He entrusted into my care. The Holy Spirit had to remind me that it was all about the Kingdom of God. This is why the Word of God made it clear in Matthew 6:33, '*...But seek first the kingdom of God and His righteousness, and all these things shall be added to you*'. It means if I am able to focus on the things of God, take Him as my first priority and pursue righteousness, then every other thing I desire will begin to gravitate towards me – including success in every area of my life. Don't get me wrong, I am not saying we should become slothful and not have dreams and aspirations, or that pursuing career and dreams are wrong. The point I am making is that everything we do on earth including our career aspirations should be in line with the will of God for our lives and tailored towards the heavenly accomplishment without compromising our faith. Needless to say, I eventually took the exam having gained divine insight. Through the help of the Holy Spirit I completed the course and graduated.

Continuing on this lecture, the Holy Spirit said, 'every human being has the potential to have a successful career while living on the earth'. Earthly success can only serve as a tool for accomplishing heavenly assignment. The moment you depart from the earth and the angels welcome you into heaven and lead you to stand before God you will not be asked about the success of your career as this is meant for earthly purposes. The question you will be asked would be more about your calling, assignment, purpose and deeds as it relates to the Kingdom of God. The Holy Spirit said, 'unfortunately, whatever career achievement you may have had or acquired cannot be reckoned with in heaven because it will be irrelevant to the Kingdom as your earthly successes cannot be transferred to heaven'.

7

God's Will on Earth as it is in Heaven

> [13] Then I heard a voice from heaven saying to me, "Write: 'Blessed are the dead who die in the Lord from now on.'" "Yes," says the Spirit, "that they may rest from their labors, and their works follow them."
> [14] Then I looked, and behold, a white cloud, and on the cloud sat One like the Son of Man, having on His head a golden crown, and in His hand a sharp sickle.
> [15] And another angel came out of the temple, crying with a loud voice to Him who sat on the cloud, "Thrust in Your sickle and reap, for the time has come for You to reap, for the harvest of the earth is ripe."
> [16] So He who sat on the cloud thrust in His sickle on the earth, and the earth was reaped.
>
> *Revelation 14:13-16*

The Holy Spirit began to shed light on the difference between Earthly Career and Heavenly Calling and which I am about to share with you.

Earthly Career

The Holy Spirit reminded me and said, 'while on earth, you may decide to study and choose a career path; you then work so hard to be successful in that career path you have chosen. As you continue to climb that ladder of success in your field of endeavour, you get rewarded for your labour and hard work. If you continue to work harder and harder, you may even become the Chief Executive Officer (CEO) of a Company, earning a huge salary and having 'fat bank balances.' The Holy Spirit said, 'when you are at that level, the world begins to distinguish you as a successful man or woman. The world begins to applaud you for your wealth, success and accomplishments.' He said, 'On the other hand, the Heavenly Calling is not quite like that.'

> [9] *"This, then, is how you should pray:*
> *"'Our Father in heaven, hallowed be your name,*
> [10] *your kingdom come, your will be done, on earth as it is in heaven.*
>
> Matthew 6:9-10 (NIV)

Heavenly Calling

The Holy Spirit said, 'when it comes to heavenly calling, you may not necessarily get paid or rewarded for what you do while on earth with earthly currency. However, there is a 'heavenly account' opened in your name and maintained on your behalf by angels who are ministering spirits assigned by God to obey our commands'. The bible states in Hebrews 1:14 **'are they not all ministering spirits sent forth to minister for those who will inherit salvation?'** Continuing, the Holy Spirit said, 'for every labour of love while here on earth for His Name sake, your heavenly account is being credited. For example, when you feed the hungry, your account gets credited, when you visit the sick and those in prison, your heavenly bank balance increases. For every act of kindness you show towards your neighbour, the homeless, the widows, the orphans, the prisoners, fatherless and so on, not out of carnality but in sincerity of your heart, you will certainly get remittance into your unseen heavenly account'.

Let me quickly make this clarification. I believe very strongly that there is a difference between your labour which is your hard work or career achievement on earth and your deeds which is your performance or actions relating to your heavenly assignment. In Revelation 14:13-16 being referred to above, it is clear that labour (toil) and deeds (legal entitlement) are not the same. It means when we die and get to heaven, we rest from our labour or toil (which remains here on earth) but we receive the reward for our deeds (which is our legal entitlement) because our deeds do follow us.

How do we inherit salvation?

I am absolutely convinced that when we finally stand before our Maker at judgment, every deed done out of love while on earth, which seemed fruitless at the time, will accordingly be rewarded in heaven. Everything will be revealed to us in our heavenly account. It is only then we will realise that our heavenly account was being credited for every heavenly transaction we made on earth as it pertains to the heavenly business. This is why the bible makes us understand in 1 Corinthians 2:9-10 that, '... *"What no eye has seen, what no ear has heard, and what no human mind has conceived the things God has prepared for those who love him—these are the things God has revealed to us by his Spirit."* Our minds cannot even comprehend the things God has in stock for us but it will all be clear when we get to meet Him on that day.

God will never forget our labour of love towards His Kingdom because He is a just God. Paul said in Hebrews

6:10 *"For God is not unjust to forget your work and labour of love which you have shown towards His name, in that you have ministered to the saints, and do minister."* Since our God is never a debtor, He cannot owe anyone. He pays a hundred fold for every bit of what we offer or give in His Name. The Bible says in Proverbs 19:17 that, *'he who is kind to the poor lends to the Lord, and He will reward him for what he has done.'* Giving to His cause is like putting your money into a savings bank account that yields huge returns.

The amount you have in your heavenly account will depend on how much hours of work you put in on earth while working in what I would call **'Heavenly Father's Business' (HFB)**. Trust me! He is the best employer of labour. His wages are fantastic and it cannot be compared to earthly rewards we receive. For example, the pay rise; the bonuses, the 'thank you' cards from our employers; awards for being the best employee of the year and so on cannot be compared to our Heavenly Father's reward. Just imagine this; if men can recognise your effort here on earth and reward you for your hard work, how much more the Most High God, the Creator of heaven and earth, who sees and knows all things including the innermost thoughts of our hearts. Why will He not reward you for your labour in His Kingdom? The bible says in Matthew 7:11 that, *"If you then, being evil, know how to give good gifts to your children, how much more shall your Father which is in heaven give good things to them that ask him?"* And God has shown us in His word that the world and all its fullness is His (Psalms 50:12a). Why go for the gift when we could go for the giver? If we take time out of our busy schedule to minister to the sick, help the poor, evangelise and visit those in prison, the angels in charge of managing our accounts in heaven will definitely be busy, crediting each of our accounts. Our God who called us is faithful. He will certainly do what He says He would do (1 Thessalonians 5:24)

Health Insurance and Pension Contributions

Just as our account in heaven is being credited, likewise our pension funds on earth are being credited through our works, for reliance upon retirement. In some companies or organisations, the amount payable on retirement depends on your last earnings or your contribution into the pension pot. You and I know that if you did not make contributions towards your pension, for example, if you opted out of the companies' pension scheme or did not work at all then, you are not likely to expect or receive much when you come up to retirement. If you are fortunate, you may be entitled to the state-pension which is just a trifling sum compared to what you would have received if you had made adequate contributions.

8

THE REWARD

⁷ I have fought the good fight, I have finished the race, I have kept the faith.
⁸ Finally, there is laid up for me the crown of righteousness, which the Lord, the righteous Judge, will give to me on that Day, and not to me only but also to all who have loved His appearing.

2 Timothy 4:7-8

Paul, in 2 Timothy 4 caught this revelation and could gladly say, '*I have fought the good fight, I have finished the race...*' He knew the reward that was ahead of him and he waited eagerly to receive it – the crown of righteousness – which God promised to give not just to Apostle Paul but to all who believe in Him. Paul knew that our God is a righteous Judge, the One who magnifies His Word more than His name (Psalms 138:2c), will surely fulfil His promise and will give to all who loved His appearing that crown of righteousness. Paul encouraged us in Hebrews 10:23 when he said, '*Let us hold fast the confession of our hope without wavering, for He who promised is faithful*'. We must never get carried away by what we see here on earth and then forget where we are going – to meet with Our Heavenly Father.

Friends, whatever we may do here on earth will be judged when we meet the King of kings. Paul the Apostle had to remind us of this fact in 2 Corinthians 5:10 when he said, *"For we must all appear before the judgment seat of Christ, so that each of us may receive what is due us for the things done while in the body, whether good or bad."* It all becomes very clear, as seen in this verse, that a day will come when we will appear before the King of kings to be judged and given rewards according to our deeds while on earth.

It means our heavenly calling is similar to the pension contributions we make in our companies or the organisation we work for on this earth. While on earth, Your Maker, the Most High God is your employer. He expects you to put in adequate contribution into your heavenly pension pot to enable you claim your entitlement when you get to heaven. The rewards you get are dependent on your contributions because He is a fair and just God. However, unlike the earthly company or organisation, your reward is not dependent on age or years of employment. This was made clear in the Bible in Matthew 20:1-16, where the parable of the workers in the vineyard is described. Both the workers who were hired first and those hired last received a denarius. Similarly, while you were on earth, if you did not put in so much towards your heavenly calling despite being saved for many years, you are not likely to get much reward as well. On the other hand, if a young believer who is just a year old in the Heavenly Father's Business puts in as much as you did within that one year, then there is a likelihood that the reward received would be the same on the last day.

If all you did on earth was, accept Jesus Christ as your Lord and Saviour, be a regular attendee in Church services, walked in righteousness, lived happily ever after and nothing more, - I can assure you that by not making effort to contribute to the Kingdom and your heavenly assignment or account, such as witnessing for souls, welfare activities etc, the most you may probably get is a party welcoming you to join the saints but with no gifts, crown or rewards. This means you were just saved by grace and did just enough to get into heaven. To me, this type of entitlement is equivalent to a state-pension. The book of James clearly sums it all up where it reminded us that *'...faith by itself, if it does not have works, is dead...'* (James 2:14-26).

You may probably consider entering heaven is all that counts most. I often hear some believers say they would gladly accept the position of a gate keeper, provided heaven is attained. I can assure you on the contrary, that you are likely to demonstrate remorse and be disappointed because of your failure to do what you were called to accomplish. To see others being presented with crown and rewards will be too painful to watch. The rewards would be too beautiful to be ignored. If you think this is not true, see what the bible says in 1 Peter 5:4, *'And when the Chief Shepherd appears, you will receive the crown of glory that will never fade away.'* This type of crown that will be given out does not fade or lose value unlike earthly rewards. Paul the Apostle had a clear understanding of this and reminded the Corinthians in 2 Corinthians 5:10 which says, **'For we must all appear before the judgment seat of Christ, that each one may receive the things** *done* **in the body,**

according to what he has done, whether good or bad. Believe me, nothing will be hidden on that day.

It will all be revealed!

I strongly believe that everything will be revealed. I wonder what our disposition will be like when a flash back of our lives is placed on a screen and a quick scan of an inscription - 'this is your life' is played back. Suddenly we will see missed opportunities to share the good news, pray for someone, neighbours we could have helped but never did. If we had obeyed that still small voice of the Holy Spirit, which would have resulted in, not only increase in God's Kingdom but also a credit to our heavenly account. Our main objective is not only to be saved but also to be a witness to as many as we can, so that they may become partakers of the salvation we have freely received. Trust me! We may not be all that happy and excited that we made heaven while our loved ones are on the other side especially after seeing the play-back on screen. Rather, it might be a case of, 'if only I had known, I would have acted differently.' It will be too late to undo what has already been done.

How do you know this, you may ask? Look at the parable of Lazarus and the Rich Man Jesus Christ shared in Luke 16:20. When the rich man requested that Lazarus be sent to his father's house to warn his brothers so that they will not come to the place of torment where he was, Abraham simply told him this was no longer possible. This is very revealing as it has provided a life lesson on how we should be mindful of our conduct while on earth.

If there was no rewards for the works done here on earth, Jesus Christ would not have said in Matthew

5:12, *'Rejoice and be exceedingly glad, for great is your reward in heaven...'*, Neither would He have warned us in Matthew 6:1 not to do our righteous deeds in public - *"Be careful not to practice your righteousness in front of others to be seen by them. If you do, you will have no reward from your Father in heaven."* In my understanding, it therefore means that because you have done your righteous deeds for men to see (that is, you deliberately allowed men to see your good deeds so that they can praise you for a job well done), you have already received the reward of men. The praise you received, which is another form of reward from men can only be received in the flesh or carnally. Then there is therefore no further reward since God looks at the heart and rewards only those things done selflessly. Hence, there will be no more credit into your heavenly account for that particular deed. Things done in the flesh or carnally are worthless in the sight of God as the scripture puts it in Romans. 8:7 - *Because the carnal mind is enmity against God; for it is not subject to the law of God, nor indeed can be.*

It does not matter how successful your earthly career is or how fat your bank balances on earth have become, if it does not line up with God's purpose and there is no remittance into your heavenly calling account as well, you will be amazed when you get to heaven that the earthly scale will tilt towards earth while the heavenly scale may be less or near empty. If that happens, it means the earthly career remittance outweighed the heavenly calling remittance. It all depends on which side of the scale you stored your treasures while on earth. However, if you were able to balance your heavenly assignment along with your earthly career, then great is your reward. You might ask, 'how can I balance my earthly career with my heavenly assignment'? The truth is that you must always ask yourself, 'does this line up with God's word and will?' In whatever you do, you must be heavenly conscious knowing that you are here on earth for a reason.

Why are you here on earth?

> [16] *You did not choose me, but I chose you and appointed you so that you might go and bear fruit—fruit that will last—and so that whatever you ask in my name the Father will give you.*
>
> *John 15:16 (NIV)*

Long before we were formed in our mother's womb, we had a purpose and were given assignments by God to fulfil while dwelling on the face of this place called earth. God made this very clear when He spoke to Prophet Jeremiah and said, **"Before I formed you in the womb I knew you, before you were born I set you apart; I appointed you as a prophet to the nations."** (Jeremiah 1:5). According to this bible passage, it is obvious that each one of us, long before we were created had been given assignments according to our gifts or talents distributed to us by God. As for Jeremiah, he was set apart to be a prophet to his nation. Does that mean we all ought to be prophets or pastors? Certainly not! God in His infinite wisdom has dispersed to everyone assignments that are unique to them. His purpose will be accomplished and everyone who executes His assignment on earth will be rewarded accordingly. This was why Paul the Apostle when writing to the Corinthians in 1 Corinthians 3:8 said, *'Now he who plants and he who waters are one, and each one will receive his own reward according to his own labor.'*

Our aim is to glorify God so that in whatever capacity we have been equipped, praise will continue to go to Him. The scripture reminded us in Colossians 3:17 saying '**And whatever you do in word or deed, do all in the name of the Lord Jesus, giving thanks to God the Father through Him**'. It is a case of being heavenly minded at all times in whatever we do.

In case you are not sure what you have been called to do, why not ask the Almighty God, Your Maker and He will reveal it to you. The word of God says in James 1:5, '**If any of you lacks wisdom, let him ask of God, who gives to all liberally and without reproach, and it will be given to him.** Also, in Matthew 7:7-8, He said, '**Ask, and it will be given to you; seek, and you will find; knock, and it will be opened to you. "For everyone who asks receives, and he who seeks finds, and to him who knocks it will be opened.**' If we diligently seek Him concerning His purpose for our lives, He will surely reveal it to us.

We are expected to bear fruits on our journey through life. Therefore, focusing on earthly career alone without a care about God's preordained purpose and assignment will be tantamount to not bearing fruit - fruit that will last (John 15:16). Earthly career and achievements are fruits but they don't last. They are temporal and cannot be transferred to heavenly accounts.

Consider the parable of the talents in the book of Matthew 25:14-32. In that chapter, we were told that the master of the house, before embarking on a long journey, gave talents to each of his servants according to their abilities. To one, he gave five talents, to another two and to another one. Each of the servants traded with their talents and made profits except the servant that received one talent. In this passage of the bible, we are told that instead of the servant with one talent trading with the masters' talent, he dug a hole in the ground and hid the master's money. When the master came back, the other two servants accounted for their talents and they were rewarded accordingly. However, the servant with the one talent returned the masters talent without trading with it and the master called him *'wicked and lazy servant'* (Matthew 25:26). In the end, even his one talent was taken away and given to the one who had ten talents. Worst still, the Bible in *verse 30* of that chapter says that the *'unprofitable servant will be cast into the outer darkness where there will be weeping and gnashing of teeth.'* The lesson I have learnt from this passage of scripture is that we are here on earth for an assignment, working in our Heavenly Father's Business which is being directed by our Heavenly Father who is the CEO and we must all give account to Him when He returns.

You are an ambassador

> [20] *Now then, we are ambassadors for Christ, as though God were pleading through us: we implore you on Christ's behalf, be reconciled to God.*
>
> 2 Corinthians 5:20

Having previously worked in the diplomatic circle, I am aware that every ambassador sent abroad is there to represent his or her country. To be regarded as a true representative of the home country, the ambassador is expected to act based on instructions and directives of the home country and report back accordingly. If for any reason the ambassador becomes oblivious of the reason for being sent to that foreign country and then begins to transact personal business or gets distracted by matters which are irrelevant to his or her assignment then that ambassador would certainly be recalled home and made to answer for any inappropriate behaviour. An ambassador, who is a true representative of his or her country, would do everything possible to please the home country.

In the same manner, every child of God is an ambassador for Christ on earth (2 Corinthians 5:20). We must call to mind that this world is not our home. We are on a journey and must represent Christ as true ambassadors until our time on earth is over. We must therefore act like those who will give account to God some day. If we truly love God, we will obey and keep His commandment. In John 14:15, Jesus Christ declared, **'If you love Me, keep My commandments.'** Let me quickly make this clear that one of the commandments Jesus Christ gave His disciples after He rose from the dead was for them to go and preach the gospel. The Bible makes clear that when He appeared to them, He *'...spoke to them, saying, 'All authority has been given to Me in heaven and on earth. Go therefore and make disciples of all the nations, baptizing them in the name of the Father and of the Son and of the Holy Spirit, teaching them to observe all things that I have commanded you; and lo, I am with you always, even to the end of the age'* (Matthew 28:18-20). This same commandment is very much applicable to every believer today. It therefore means that our first assignment as an employee of Heavenly Fathers Business is soul winning. In Proverbs 11:30, the Bible says, **'the fruit of the righteous is a tree of life. And he who wins souls is wise.'**

Going back to my previous analysis of pension contribution, it is clear that in order to draw from your pension fund, you would first have to be in retirement. Just like the parable of the talents, the servants did not know their fate until after a long wait when their master finally returned to settle accounts with them. Similarly, for you to see how much you have in your heavenly account and know what your reward would be, your work on earth would have been completed and you would have to stand before your Maker in heaven. It is only then will all be revealed whether your account is in the black or in the red. Unfortunately, there is no overdraft facility in heaven neither IOUs ("I owe you"). Jesus Christ made it clear to us in the scripture when he said, *"...behold I am coming quickly, and My reward is with Me, to give to everyone according to his work"* (Revelation 22:12). My earnest prayer for you and I is that when we stand before the King of kings , the only one who has our reward in His hands, you and I will be able to give a good account of how well we spent our talents. Thereafter, you and I will receive our just reward according to our works and we will hear '**well done, good and faithful servant'** (Matthew 25:21 & 23) and at the same time, we will be able to enter into the joy of our Father's rest.

But who are you working for?

It is whoever you work for that you will collect your retirement income from. You cannot work for Mr. A and go to Mr. B after retirement to demand for your retirement income. Even if you were bold enough to approach Mr. B, he would politely tell you that you were never his employee and as a result, you are not entitled to any pension from his establishment.

As the master told his servants in Matthew 25:21, *"well done, good and faithful servant....enter into the joy of your lord"* I believe this same principle will apply to us regarding our heavenly assignment. I am so certain that our heavenly Father will welcome everyone who 'traded' or 'worked' in the 'Heavenly Fathers Business' according to the instruction of our God. We ought to have put in so much to expect a just reward. I am persuaded that Paul, the Apostle caught a glimpse of the great reward that awaited him in heaven and he was so convinced of his work that he could say, *"I have fought the good fight, I have finished the race, I have kept the faith. Finally there is laid up for me the crown of righteousness, which the Lord, the righteous Judge, will give to me on that Day, and not to me only but also to all who have loved His appearing"* (2 *Timothy 4:7-9)(emphasis by me)*. Paul did not just finish the race; he also fought the good fight and kept the faith. Therefore He could boldly say, **'For to me, to live is Christ and to die is gain'** (Philippians 1:21). Paul would rather be in heaven because he realised the greater glory awaited him however, his passion for God's work made him choose to remain here on earth a little longer for the sake of the people he was called to preach to, so he could finish his assignment. The more he worked on earth, the more his heavenly account was being credited (mansion and stars on his crown etc). Equally, each one of us ought to be diligent and faithful in keeping our Heavenly Fathers Business so we too can boldly say like Paul, *'...to live is Christ and to die is gain* (Philippians 1:21).'

In the past, I wondered and asked questions on why Jesus Christ told those 'workers' in Matthew 7:21-23 that He never knew them? I used to ponder over His reasons for telling them, **"depart from Me, you workers of iniquity"**. In reality, they were workers too. But now I know why. It is similar to my analysis in the previous paragraph of a man who worked for Mr A but after retirement, he then went to demand for his pension contribution from Mr B. The truth is that, this worker actually worked but not for Mr. B, as a result, he was demanding for his rewards from the wrong employer. Just as Mr. B would calmly tell him, 'sorry I have never met you because you never worked for me' so also will Jesus Christ tell every worker of iniquity who claim to be working in the Lord's vineyard but are not.

My prayer is that our work on earth will stand the test of fire at judgment and we will only hear 'well done' from Our Father in heaven.

9
HOW MUCH TIME DO YOU THINK YOU HAVE LEFT?

> *⁴ I must work the works of Him who sent Me while it is day; the night is coming when no one can work.*
> *⁵ As long as I am in the world, I am the light of the world."*
>
> John 9:4-5

Dear brothers and sisters, it is very important for us to know how to work in this vineyard of Our God called 'Heavenly Father's Business'. Paul warned us in 1 Thessalonians 4:4 that each of us should know how to possess his own vessel in sanctification and honour. Paul also advised us in 2 Timothy 4:5 about the importance of accomplishing our task here on earth when he said to Timothy *"But you be watchful in all things, endure afflictions, do the work of an evangelist, fulfil your ministry."*

As an employee, while in employment you are expected to have made adequate contribution towards your pension fund long before you reach your retirement age. You cannot inform your previous employer, when you are already in retirement that you wish to return and make more contributions towards your retirement. It will be too late to do so. Even so, your heavenly account can only be credited while we are still here on earth. Unfortunately, it cannot be credited when our work on earth is over and we are already standing before our Maker in heaven. As mentioned earlier, there is no overdraft facility when we get to heaven neither IOUs ("I owe you"). It is a case of what you are worth is what you get. We must also bear in mind that each one of us has different number of days assigned to us on earth after which we must give an account on how well we spent the days assigned to us. Some have a short time on earth to finish their task while others live longer. But whether we live for a short time or longer, we must learn to spend our days wisely in accordance with God's plan and purpose. Psalms 90:12 says, **'So teach us to number our days, that we may gain a heart of wisdom.'**

Jesus, while He was here on earth, knew His purpose and assignment so He did all He needed to do within the time frame and completed His work – the redemption of man. He was conscious of this fact that was why He said in the Scriptures – *"I must work the works of Him who sent Me while it is day; the night is coming when no one can work. As long as I am in the world, I am the light of the world."* (John 9:4-5). His task was to do the will of the heavenly Father not His own will. He is telling us the same today through His Word that just as the Father had sent Him, He also has sent us (John 20:21) that we should go and bear fruits, not just mere fruits but fruits that will last (John 15:16). How else can we bear fruits? Unless we first sow that seed which God has already given to each one of us long before we were born (see Jeremiah 1:5). All we need do is plant the seed so that we would reap a bountiful harvest on the last day. A farmer can only reap during harvest season. However, if the farmer refuses to sow during the season of planting, he would have nothing to reap during harvest season. Similarly, while on earth (which is our season of planting), we must do all we are required and assigned to do in order to reap the harvest of what we have planted in heaven. Remember, the first seed to sow is always the seed of salvation which is soul-winning. We have this clear commandment in the Bible in Matthew 28:18-20 which says *'And Jesus came and spoke to them, saying, "All authority has been given to Me in heaven and on earth. Go therefore and make disciples of all the nations, baptizing them in the name of the Father and of the Son and of the Holy Spirit, teaching them to observe all things that I have commanded you; and lo, I am with you always, even to the end of the age." Amen.*

In this Bible passage above, there are no exceptions. Whether we are rich, poor, young or old, we are commanded to teach others about the love of God that compelled Him to send His only begotten Son, Jesus Christ, to die on the cross for our sins. We are expected to do this within our circle of influence. Our current location is always our field and we are to plough it until we are called home to answer on how we managed that field.

Jesus Christ laid down these examples when He went about achieving His earthly career. In Acts 10:38, the Bible says, '**how God anointed Jesus of Nazareth with the Holy Spirit and with power, who went about doing good and healing all who were oppressed by the devil, for God was with Him.**' He did so many miracles and signs and wonders followed Him and He cast out demons. In Mark 6:3, He was even referred to as 'the carpenter'. However, that was not His only purpose for coming to the earth. His coming was not only to open blind eyes, heal the sick, cast out demons and feed the multitude neither was He on earth to pursue a professional career in carpentry rather, His purpose and assignment was to reconcile man back to God. That was His main assignment - to redeem mankind to his original state – A state of redemption, restoration and relationship with God the Father.

Jesus brought man back to the original state of authority and victory over the works of the devil. Jesus died a balanced death on the cross in order to link us back to the Father (spirit-soul-body). In the course of reconciling us back to the Father, Jesus had compassion on the sick and healed them and even raised the dead. His compassion to heal the sick did not override His vision to bring salvation to all mankind. He was able to balance His earthly career with His heavenly assignment – the vision of the Father, the will of our God - When He rose again the third day, He completed the work. The cross on which Jesus Christ died became a balanced scale that is not tilted at an angle. When Jesus Christ hung on the cross, He said, *'it is finished'* (John 19:30) meaning His work of reconnecting man back to the Father had been accomplished. It means 'paid for in full', it means task has been completed and the victory was right there and then handed back to mankind. That is the foundation on which we stand as children of God and upon which we must continue to build – the finished work of Our Lord Jesus Christ. He then commanded us to go and preach the gospel to all men so that through His name, whoever believes in Him will receive remission of sins (Acts 10:40-43).

What if there was no cross?

> ¹ There is therefore now no condemnation to those who are in Christ Jesus,[a] who do not walk according to the flesh, but according to the Spirit.
> ² For the law of the Spirit of life in Christ Jesus has made me free from the law of sin and death.
> ³ For what the law could not do in that it was weak through the flesh, God did by sending His own Son in the likeness of sinful flesh, on account of sin: He condemned sin in the flesh,
> ⁴ that the righteous requirement of the law might be fulfilled in us who do not walk according to the flesh but according to the Spirit.
> ⁵ For those who live according to the flesh set their minds on the things of the flesh, but those who live according to the Spirit, the things of the Spirit.
>
> Romans 8:1-5

As Jesus Christ did not only come to heal and raise the dead but to reconcile man back to God even so, we are not here just to fulfil our earthly career. Imagine what would have happened if Jesus had decided to pursue His career in carpentry instead or focus solely on the earthly ministry of healing the sick and working miracles without going to the cross for you and I.

Have you also considered what would have happened if Jesus had been distracted by falling for the trick of the devil when He was tempted and commanded to turn stone into bread? (See Matthew chapter 4). He probably would not have fulfilled His Heavenly Father's Business which was His original assignment and purpose. There would have been no redemption for mankind and as a result, there would have been no salvation, no restoration and relationship between God and man. But, in humility and obedience, Jesus kept His eyes fixed on the assignment without losing focus and He paid the price even the price of death on the cross. Why? Because that was the reason He came. The Bible in Philippians 2:8 says that Jesus Christ, '...*being found in appearance as a man, He humbled Himself by becoming obedient to death—even death on a cross!* As a result of one man's obedience to His heavenly calling, redemption came to mankind. It is so profound in that Jesus finished the work and took His place, seated at the right hand of the Father in heaven. (Mark 16:19; Hebrews 12:2; Philippians. 2:8-9). What have you been called to do? Have you obeyed or are you being distracted by earthly matters?

What you set your eyes on matter

> *⁴ Do not weary yourself to gain wealth, Cease from your consideration of it.*
> *⁵ When you set your eyes on it, it is gone. For wealth certainly makes itself wings Like an eagle that flies toward the heavens.*
>
> *Proverbs 23:4-5 (NASB)*

You may have been very successful career-wise and become rich financially because of your hard work. However, if you did not work for your heavenly Father to guarantee your pension in your heavenly account, you will be so stunned when you get to heaven to discover that nothing is in your heavenly account. I strongly believe that not much will be said about our career on earth, neither would our earthly bank balances be reckoned with when we stand before God on that judgment day. The Bible made it very clear in 2 Corinthians 5:10 where it says, *"For we must all appear before the judgment seat of Christ, so that each of us may receive what is due us for the things done while in the body, whether good or bad"*. I am absolutely certain that all that will be asked or said will be about our kingdom work as it relates to heavenly assignment.

The Bible is our life manual and made it very clear in Matthew 6:33 – *"But seek first the kingdom of God and His righteousness, and all these things shall be added to you."* The truth of the matter is, if we dare to shift our focus to the things of the Kingdom and chase after His righteousness, then all **the things which we chase after** will begin to gravitate towards us like a magnet. It is God's principle which has already been set in place and will certainly come to pass if we obey this principle.

Nothing on earth is permanent

The Word of God makes us understand that earthly wealth does have wings and they can fly but heavenly savings are like treasures stored away in a secure safe. That is why Jesus warns us in Matthew 6:19-21 *"Do not lay up for yourselves treasures on earth, where moth and rust destroy and where thieves break in and steal; but lay up for yourselves treasures in heaven, where neither moth nor rust destroys and where thieves do not break in and steal. For where your treasure is, there your heart will be also."*

I would like to clarify this point, wealth in itself is not a sin after all the Bible talks about the cattle on a thousand hills belonging to our Father including the silver and gold - they are all His (Psalms 50:10-12; Haggai 2:8). The Bible also states in 2 Corinthians 8:9 that Jesus Christ became poor so that through His poverty we might become rich. Therefore, we who are heirs and joint heirs with Christ ought to have access to everything that belongs to our Father and our Lord Jesus Christ (Romans 8:17; Galatians 3:29). However, there is a problem if as a result of our wealth we begin to live and behave as though the earth is our final destination without caring about the things of God. This is where the biggest challenge lies – balancing earthly pursuits of wealth and the things of God's Kingdom. I believe this is one of the reasons why Jesus, in Mark 10:23-24 said that, **it is hard for a rich man to enter into the kingdom of heaven.** Why is this the case? It is simply because our faith is now on what our wealth can give and not what Jesus can provide through faith in Him. It means we place our wealth first and Jesus becomes second in our order of priority. A good look at what Jesus said gives us clarity of it all *"No one can serve two masters. For you will hate one and love the other; you will be devoted to one and despise the other. You cannot serve both God and money"* (Matthew 6:24 NLT).

We must remember at every point of our lives that our wealth is given to us not only for our benefit but also to serve as a blessing to others. The Lord gave us this example in the scripture through the life of Abraham when He first called him in Genesis 12:1-2, *'The LORD had said to Abram, "Leave your native country, your relatives, and your father's family, and go to the land that I will show you. I will make you into a great nation. I will bless you and make you famous, and you will be a blessing to others..."* The reason God blessed Abram was for him to become a blessing to nations. Our wealth or possessions on earth is given to us for the fulfilment of our heavenly assignment.

Another example in the Bible of how God blesses us so that we can be a blessing is found in the story of Joseph in Genesis 41. Joseph became the Prime Minister of Egypt, commanding the wealth of the whole nation. The reasoning behind his promotion was tied to the preservation of the lives of his family during famine and ultimately the fulfilment of God's will and purpose concerning the children of Israel (see Genesis Chapters 45 & 46). Our earthly career and heavenly calling is intertwined to the degree of our earthly career being the vehicle for accomplishing the heavenly call. Our earthly career success should therefore not be taken in isolation. We are blessed so that we can be a blessing.

In the book of Deuteronomy, Moses kept reminding the children of Israel on their way to the Promise Land not to forget their God when they become wealthy in case they forget and begin to think that it is their power and might that made them wealthy. He said to the children of Israel, *"And you shall remember the Lord your God, for it is He who gives you power to get wealth, that He may establish His covenant which He swore to your fathers, as it is this day"* (Deuteronomy 8:18). He repeatedly warned them that the reason God blessed them was to establish His covenant which He made to their forefathers (Genesis 12:1-2). We should never get to that point where we believe that our blessing is for our household to consume just for pleasure – Never!

10
BE RICH TOWARDS GOD, THERE LIES YOUR GUARANTEE

> [19] *And I will say to my soul, "Soul, you have many goods laid up for many years; take your ease; eat, drink, and be merry."'*
> [20] *But God said to him, 'Fool! This night your soul will be required of you; then whose will those things be which you have provided?'*
> [21] *"So is he who lays up treasure for himself, and is not rich toward God."*
>
> Luke 12:19-21

Take a look at this interesting parable of the rich fool in Luke 12:13-21. In the parable, Jesus cautioned us to beware of covetousness because life is not all about abundance of wealth and possession. All can be taken away in a flash including our own life because He is the giver of all things. But if we are rich towards God and remember that He owns all things including the breath in our nostrils, then our treasure is secured in heaven.

We can remember in 2008, not too long ago the world's economy took a downturn for which nations are still struggling to recover. Great nations who trusted in their economy, shares and stock market, property market boom, etc woke up one morning and came to the realisation that they had lost everything overnight. Why was the world in shock? It is because there had been so much trust in the market systems that no one ever imagined it would fail at that point in time. The scripture in 1 Timothy. 6:17 (NLT) puts it cautiously when it said, *'Teach those who are rich in this world not to be proud and not to trust in their money, which is so unreliable. Their trust should be in God, who richly gives us all we need for our enjoyment.'* Jeremiah 49:4 also says, **'Why do you boast of your valleys, O faithless daughter, who trusted in her treasures, saying, 'Who will come against me?'** We ought to remember that it is the word of God that holds this world together and He didn't create us just so we can accumulate wealth on earth and forget all about heaven.

God, the Creator of heaven and earth, knows that our earthly career only leads to earthly reward which is temporary but our heavenly calling leads to permanent eternal reward. Every earthly achievement or riches is like a thick winter coat needed to protect us from the cold winter. Once the winter is over and the summer is here, we no longer need the winter coat because it will be too hot to put on. The same is applicable to our earthly career achievements and riches. It is needed to make us live comfortable lives while in the body and to serve as a tool in accomplishing our heavenly assignment.

Life is but a vapour

> *[13] Now listen, you who say, "Today or tomorrow we will go to this or that city, spend a year there, carry on business and make money."*
> *[14] Why, you do not even know what will happen tomorrow. What is your life? You are a mist that appears for a little*

while and then vanishes."

James 4:13-14

When our lives on earth are over, we are expected to pull off our 'earthly coat' - worldly possessions - and put on our 'heavenly coat' that is, our deeds as it relates to our heavenly calling and assignment. Everything we have ever worked for while on earth cannot be taken to heaven. The houses, the cars, the clothes, and qualifications etc, all these things, good as they may seem, will have to be left behind because they are not useful when we get to heaven.

Recently, my dearly beloved mother went to be with the Lord at the ripe age of ninety-five. At the funeral, the whole family gathered together to pay her their last respects. As her body was being laid to rest, all she had on was that lovely white cotton lace. Everything she ever owned during her ninety-five years of living was left behind. None of her possessions were taken along with her or carried to the grave. As I watched the interment process, it drove the point home again that of a truth, we came to this world with no material possessions and we all will also return without any. Just as King Solomon puts it where he said, *"Everyone comes naked from their mother's womb, and as everyone comes, so they depart. They take nothing from their toil that they can carry in their hands"* (Ecclesiastes 5:15).

What do you value most presently?

The questions I would like to ask now and which I often ask myself also are these:

1. What are the most important things in your life at present?

2. Will the things you currently do count towards your heavenly reward or will it just be for earthly reward?

3. Have you become so earthly conscious that you have completely forgotten all about heaven?

4. Do your daily decisions boost your heavenly account or your earthly account?

5. What have you been called to do? Are you presently on track or have you become distracted?

6. If not sure what you have been called to do, have you taken time to ask your Maker – the One who created you?

The answers you give to these questions will determine where your priority lies. I believe strongly that what we will be asked when we get to heaven are mainly how we managed our heavenly assignment, and the people we were assigned to minister to. I do not want to be misunderstood. When I say, 'the people you were assigned to minister to' I am not just referring to pulpit ministry alone, far from it. Everyone is not called to minister on the pulpit. Your calling could be to the people in your workplace to make sure that your light shines in that environment for all to see. By merely observing your lifestyle they may all give their lives to Christ and glorify your Father in heaven. However, if all you do is get to the office, do your job but are careless about the people around you, then you have not allowed your light to shine. Your calling could take on different outward expressions. For example, you may have to minister to your neighbour who has matrimonial issues and from time to time comes to you for advice. You know too well that God has blessed you with words of wisdom and you are so good at encouraging others.

Even a simple smile could change the life of somebody who is emotionally depressed and that smile could make the difference in that person's life.

Christians are the Bible being read daily by the world because you may never have the opportunity to open the scriptures and preach from it but a believers' lifestyle preaches more than the Bible. It can either win or discourage others from accepting Jesus Christ. It is that simple. It is your light that will shine and make men see your good works and glorify the Father in heaven (Matthew 5:16). Just like the parable of the talents, it will be a question of whether the people God assigned to us to care for have been well catered for. In the final analysis, it will be an issue of whether we actually traded with our given talents and fulfilled our purpose on earth.

I have never stopped imagining how it will be like on that day. I bet there will be surprises! The shock will be even more if on that day we see people we hardly spoke to just because they were not in our league of friends or from our ethnic background. Those we felt we were more righteous than, claiming their rewards for a job well done and in the end sitting at the feet of Jesus Christ. And on the other side, we see those we rubbed shoulders with, those we celebrated and applauded - because they had titles and belonged to a certain league - being told to depart for being workers of iniquity. It will be a great surprise especially if they were people we believed in or thought they were working for the Kingdom of God, so we followed them rather than follow Jesus even though we knew Jesus made it clear that He is the Way, the Truth and the Light (**John 14:6**). We were so mesmerised by their looks, eloquence and charisma, that we forgot ourselves and began to walk by sight instead of by faith without searching the scriptures to find out the truth for ourselves. We forgot to imitate the people of Berea in Acts 17:11 who received the word with all readiness, and searched the Scriptures daily to find out whether what Paul and Silas were preaching to them about Jesus was true. We forgot about the Word of God where it clearly warned us saying **'you shall know the truth, and the truth shall set you free'** (John 8:32). May the Almighty God help our understanding and may we never lose focus or take our eyes off our Lord and Saviour, Jesus Christ, Amen.

Apostle Peter gave us this advice when he wrote in 2 Peter 1:10-11 that we should even be more diligent to make our calling and election sure because it is only in so doing that we will never stumble. He said, **'an entrance will be supplied to us in abundance into the everlasting Kingdom of our Lord and Saviour Jesus Christ'.**

I believe what Apostle Peter meant was that if you lay up for yourselves treasures in heaven by fulfilling God's assignment on earth, which is your heavenly calling, what you are actually doing is opening the doors of your heavenly accounts. As you continue to fulfil God's agenda, you are guaranteeing yourself a perpetual access into the everlasting Kingdom of our Lord and Saviour Jesus Christ. Your account in heaven can never be in red neither will you lack anything on earth because the more you put in, the more doors of opportunity will be opened to you simply because you have put God first before earthly things. In Luke 12:31 Jesus told the disciples to seek first the kingdom of God and all other things will be added to them.

Therefore, we ought to set our minds on our heavenly

calling not on earthly things alone so that 'when the Chief Shepherd appears' we 'will receive the crown of glory that does not fade away'(paraphrased) (1 Peter 5:4). Apostle Paul told the Colossians to set their minds on heavenly things not on earthly things because earthly things should no longer have value to them since they are dead to those things and are now hidden with Christ Jesus in God. When Christ who is our life appears, then we also will appear with Him in glory (Colossians 3:1-4). He also sounded the same warning to the Philippians that they should not follow those who set their minds on earthly things as their primary concern is self gratification. Instead, they were advised to follow the godly pattern because their **citizenship is in heaven** (not on earth!) (Philippians 3:17-20).

The three parables about the Kingdom

Even though we have never been to heaven before, Jesus painted a vivid picture of what it looks like in these parables He told the disciples in Matthew 13:44-52.

Jesus Christ likened the Kingdom of heaven to a treasure hidden in the field; beautiful pearls or a dragnet cast into the sea. A closer look at the dictionary definition of each of these key words will give us a clearer picture. The Oxford Dictionary defines a treasure as *a quantity of precious metals, gems, or other valuable objects*; Pearls was being referred to as a highly priced and precious thing, a gem while a dragnet is described as mainly used to hunt, an apparatus for dredging or recovering something drowned – a net drawn through a river or across.

From the three descriptions, it is clear that as children of God, we ought to have our focus on the Kingdom of heaven based on the description given to us by Jesus.

If we truly believe the account of Jesus Christ, then we must accept the fact that a great price awaits us in heaven. It may seem as though it is hidden from us and we would have to seek diligently after it, however, we must have that assurance that He who promised is faithful (Hebrews 10:23) and would surely reward us at the appointed time.

The things God has prepared for His saints have been revealed in His word through the help of the Holy Spirit. The Bible makes it clear that eyes has not seen it neither has ear heard it (1 Corinthians 2:9-12). If we take into account the heavenly agenda in whatever we do, it means we are banking into that heavenly account for which we do not physically see at the moment but will be revealed to us on that Day. In 1 Corinthians 3:13-14 Paul said, *'each one's work will become clear; for the Day will declare it, because it will be revealed by fire; and the fire will test each one's work, of what sort it is. If anyone's work which he has built on it endures, he will receive a reward'*.

May we receive our just reward on that day in Jesus name. However, in order to receive our reward, there is the need to balance and align whatever we do with heavens agenda.

11

THE BALANCING ACT

⁷ There is one who makes himself rich, yet has nothing; And one who makes himself poor, yet has great riches.

(Proverbs 13:7)

As followers of Jesus Christ, the cross is the only scale that can give us the most accurate measurement in our quest of achieving a balance in the pursuit of an earthly career alongside our heavenly calling. 1 Peter 2:21 puts this rightly when it says,' **For to this you were called, because Christ also suffered for us, leaving us an example, that you should follow His steps.'**

We will miss the greatest reward if we equate our heavenly assignment with our earthly career because God does not reward the way the world rewards. The Bible in 1 Corinthians 1:27 says that God chose those things the world considers foolish in order to shame those who think they are wise. It means those things the world considers as senseless are the very things God uses to glorify His name. This passage in Isaiah 55:8-9 states succinctly, '**For My thoughts are not your thoughts, Nor are your ways My ways, "says the Lord.**

For as the heavens are higher than the earth, so are My ways higher than your ways, and My thoughts than your thoughts.' Otherwise, how can we reconcile the parable of the lost sheep (Matthew 18:12) and the lost coin (Luke 15:8-10)? Would it not have been more sensible in the eyes of men to stay with the ninety-nine instead of going after just one?

Earthly career rewards by setting us on a platform where much gain, greater result and rewards, success, achievements and instant recognition are expected. We are celebrated as being successful when this becomes the case. Conversely, heavenly calling is not quite like that. God may for instance call and bless a minister of the gospel with ten members for a congregation for a start. This number may likely remain so for a considerable number of years longer than expected by the minister. On the other hand, a second minister with congregational members of one hundred within a short period of time, arriving on the scene long after the first minister is considered the most successful anointed man or woman of God, while the ten-member minister would be looked at scornfully. For some, the one with the ten member congregation is regarded as not growing and an unanointed Church. The exciting aspect is that God's ways are not ours. That was why He said *'For where two or three are gathered together in My Name, I am there in the midst of them'* (Matthew 18:20). If God was so much into numbers before releasing His anointing He would have said 'where billions and billions are gathered together in My Name, there am I in the midst of them.' To God be all the glory because He is not into numbers like we consider numbers. May I dare say that if you are a minister of the gospel with a small congregation; keep rejoicing because in His own appointed time, He will add to the numbers as He wills. The book of Ecclesiastes 3:11 says, **'He has made everything beautiful in its time.'**

To further buttress this that God can reveal His might even with small rather than a large number for His name to be glorified, take a look at the story in Judges Chapter 7. Isn't it amazing how God decided to use only three hundred men instead of ten thousand to give the Israelites victory over the Midianites? It is the unity of minds and faith towards God that counts. The Bible also makes it clear in 2 Peter 3:8 that with God one day is a thousand years and a thousand years are a day. The things men approve and applaud may not have been approved by God because He looks at the heart and not the outward appearance.

In 1 Samuel 16:1 - 7, when Saul sinned against God by disobeying the Lord's command regarding the Amalekites, the Lord rejected him as king instantly. In the eyes of the people, he was still king. The Lord said to Samuel not to consider Saul's appearance or height because He (God) had already rejected him.

The truth is that, as you serve faithfully even in the little God has placed in your care, in due season, if you do not faint, He will reward you accordingly just like the parable of the talents (Matthew 25:14-30). God is interested in us demonstrating faithfulness and obedience in little things before committing bigger things into our hands. This can sometimes be delayed for our good. He knows that we need patience, perseverance and tenacity in our journey through life. Behind the scene, in our waiting period, He is moulding our character and teaching us integrity because He is interested in our finished work rather than the half baked product. Every time we complete a task no matter how little, the reward for our faithfulness is credited into our heavenly account.

Bearing in mind that our ultimate goal is heaven, we must be conscious of our conducts at all times and be focused. Don't be deceived by the temporary glamour of this world. There is no act of service we do on earth in His Name that will not be rewarded. In the end, all will be revealed when we get to heaven.

Whereas, earthly career seeks maximum benefit, on the other hand heavenly calling rejoices over the smallest contribution made towards heavenly assignment.

Invest in eternity!

If there will be no reward for our work on earth, Jesus would not have given us His promise in Revelation 22:12 where He said, *'And behold, I am coming quickly, and My reward is with Me, to give to everyone according to his work.'*

Remember, God is not a man to tell lies neither will He change His mind concerning His promises. The Word of God gives us this assurance. *'God is not a man, so He does not lie. He is not human, so He does not change His mind. Has He ever spoken and failed to act? Has He ever promised and not carried it through?'* (Numbers 23:19) (NLT). Whenever God makes a promise, He will surely fulfil it. In Isaiah 55:11, God said, *'So shall My word be that goes forth from My mouth; it shall not return to Me void, but it shall accomplish what I please, and it shall prosper in the thing for which I sent it'.*

My prayer for you is that from this day forth, you begin to live and breathe for eternity if you have not already been doing so. In due course, when you get to meet with the King of kings, you will be glad you did. You will then hear, 'well done thou good and faithful servant.'

May God's will be done on earth as it is in heaven.

'In this manner, therefore, pray: Our Father in heaven, Hallowed be Your Name. Your kingdom come, Your will be done on earth as it is in heaven' – Matthew 6:9-10

A Simple Prayer

All these heavenly rewards I talked about in this book do not come to us unless we have a personal relationship with Our Lord and Saviour Jesus Christ. It is never too late to join the family of God. I am not talking about religion or church but a personal relationship with Our Lord and Saviour Jesus Christ.

If you would like to receive Him as Lord over your life today, would you repeat this prayer?

> *'Heavenly Father, I confess that I am a sinner. Have mercy on me and forgive me of all of my sins. From today, I believe that your word is true and that You sent your son, Jesus Christ to die on the cross for my sins. I believe that His blood washed me clean from all unrighteousness. I believe that on the third day He rose from the dead. Lord Jesus, come into my heart and be my personal Lord and Saviour. I give you my life and ask that You take absolute control from this moment on. I believe my sins are forgiven and I am now born again. I thank you for saving me. In Jesus Christ Name I pray, Amen.*

If you prayed this prayer, I believe you are now 'born again'. I encourage you to find and attend a bible-believing church near you so that you will have that firm foundation in God.

If you are not sure what to do after this prayer or you have any question, feel free to contact me. I would love to hear from you. You can write using the email address below.

Email: phil.ikon@yahoo.com

www.ingramcontent.com/pod-product-compliance
Lightning Source LLC
Chambersburg PA
CBHW020017050426
42450CB00005B/516